pack light

the title of this book was inspired by
lyrics i've been quietly singing to myself for two decades:

"one day all them bags gon' get in your way, so pack light"
(Erykah Badu, Bag Lady)

pack light

poems, prose, and untold stories

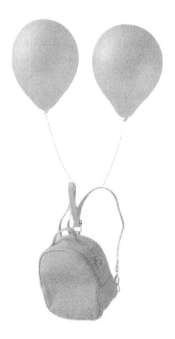

tiffany rose

www.rosewithwords.com

For rights, permissions, and bulk order information please contact:
tiffany rose
rosewithwords@gmail.com

ISBN: 979-8-9885562-4-4 (Paperback)

Library of Congress Control Number:
2023910832

Cover/Book design by tiffany rose

First printing edition 2023.

www.rosewithwords.com

for Chi Chi
who changed her stars
and birthed a galaxy
with no roadmap,
thank you for your heart.

for Marguerite Annie,
the most singin'-est
songbird of them all,
thank you for the stories.

and to anyone in the thick of survival
or somewhere along the journey
home to themselves,

keep going.

some gps:

the words that follow were written in an effort
to revisit voiceless versions of myself, sit with them for a spell,
and after too many decades, give them the chance to speak.

this collection started as a writing ritual,
gentle passage into the past in an effort to release
untold truths manifesting as creative blocks.

it turned into an exploration through my first 18 years.
pieces of the remembering, the loving, the praying,
the questioning, the surviving, the hurting, the healing
packed into pages and placed here in your hands.

this is by no means the entire story,
but a wise witch once said,

"it's always best to start at the beginning."
—Glinda the Good Witch, a personal hero

there is some material relating to:

grief / trauma / sexual assault / addiction / racism
abuse / violence / mental illness and possibly more.

please take care of yourself.

and remember,
the girl speaking on the following pages
time traveled to tell you these stories
from a safe and sturdy place.

"the truth is you never can leave home.
you take it with you everywhere you go.
it's under your skin. it moves the tongue or slows it,
colors the thinking, impedes upon the logic."

–*Maya Angelou*

act

1

made to be each others

i believe i was born
in the dreams of a girl named chi-chi
maybe i heard her prayers on those days
she was locked out of her house
told to fend for herself, find her own way
maybe she called out, i heard
and chose her way back then

maybe that's why i love
'60s silhouettes and Motown sounds
because that's when the idea of me was planted
somewhere in the great before
i heard the cry of a forgotten girl
who just wanted to belong
to someone and be loved entirely

and because little chi-chi
had magic no one bothered to see
she conjured me
with a fierce love and devotion
to something big and beautiful
maybe i heard her call and thought

> *yes, her.*
> *i'd like to be hers*
> *and have her as mine.*

consecration

i was baptized
in the same church
that wouldn't marry my parents

a romantic merger
isn't worth risking it all
but i guess the birth of god's baby is.

it is a complicated thing
to be born with brown skin
and a beaming Black heart
in the american south
to know the inner workings
and delusions of supremacy
so intimately
and still find the meeting
of lily white arms
where a carefully pieced-together
golden heart beats
a song written just for me
to be the safest home
i have ever known.

–there's no place like my mother's arms

when i was a baby
my grandma wouldn't visit inside

instead, she would watch
through parted curtains from the car

she has lived long enough to know
that whiteness can live in the walls

she has lived long enough to know better
than to get caught between its corners

—no matter how much it looks like love

show + tell

my mama gave me a Josephine Baker poster
for my birthday because i love me some her
she's about the prettiest lady i've ever seen
and a little odd too, like me, i can tell
my mama smiles real wide when i'm excited
but i think she's sad too
maybe because me and Miss Baker
look more like we some kin than me and her
but that's not even all the way true
i got my mama hands and her smile
we even laugh the same
i see it sometimes but most folks don't
like that white lady who snatched my arm in Winn Dixie
thinking i was bothering the same body that made me
but mama set that lady straight real quick
and she always make sure i see the me she can't be
in brown skin ladies on TV and album covers
or my dance teacher and the lady
who hot combs my hair for Easter
since we moved and now my aunties live a long drive away
so now i got my poster and my Flo Jo barbie doll
and we listen to Sade and Tina Turner on Saturday morning
i dress up in mama nightgowns and her worn out work heels
and play pretend when i'm supposed to help clean up
and it make me feel better about what that red-headed girl
said on the bus

>   *"my mama said you, your mama,*
>   *and your daddy is an abomination."*

maybe i should take my poster and doll to school
show and tell that nasty girl that nothing this beautiful
could be anything other than holy.

deep down in muddy waters

we paint our ceilings blue to keep the evil spirits at bay. we say things like *glory be* and ask *where your people from.* we know what outside smells like when it sticks to skin and feel the rain coming in the crook of our knees. we eat every part, including the neck, pick and shell the peas with the same fingertips we use to grease scalps and pull switches from trees. we shuck oysters, boil crabs and wash greens, cover tables with white lace dollies and couches with sticky plastic sleeves. these are my grandmother's things and her mama's things and her mama's things and her misses things from when strong backs and staunch spirits carried things down the coast through the muck and wide open fields to factories and wrapped porches with blue ceilings and white kitchens in search of homes with growing rows and room for beds and everlasting florida water.

a hymn for grandma

Mahalia Jackson plays through the walls
her stories and jeopardy live inside the screen
giant silver pots simmer ham hock laced greens
next to little bowls of soft, solid grease
freshly washed batches of picked peas
poured from crinkled plastic grocery bags
tattered, filled-to-the-brim address books
and a worn marked-up bible at the head of the bed
the smell of mothballs and perfumed powder
sifting through the senses of neighbors
and storytellers and deacons and do-gooders
that come to commune in the front room
fresh clothes held by wooden pins on a line
just outside the sky-wide shade of the pecan tree
next to never-ending honeysuckle vines
and scraps for stray dogs she pretends to despise
daily evening perches on the front porch
a tiny giant in sweet house shoes
at the top of her hill, wondering

how did i make it over.

tender headed

[ten-der-heh-ded]
adjective
1. too soft for strong hands.
2. too difficult to be held for long; inconvenient.

whatever it means
i don't want to be anymore
because i want to stay
in my grandma's hands forever
and whatever it means
makes me too hard to hold.

grandma gives directions
the same way she cooks
no measurements or mile markers
just memory and knowing
in her bones

she don't need recipes
when she lived more life
than pages in them cookbooks

got more direction
from prayers and pulpits
than any map.

—grandma got a compass for hands

the summer of '87

i don't remember the day
you showed up
i just know everything changed
when you did
all the colors got brighter
the songs sweeter

i thought you must be a babydoll
because mom said
she made you for me
our same brown skin and curly hair
surely you were sent
to be mine

some girls get to keep
their dads
but i got to keep you
my brother

and maybe that's even better
because you won't leave
and i know you already love me
by the way you
squeeze my finger so
maybe you won't want to

you will be where
i store my love
when it can't
live inside me
you are
the very best thing.

mama, the mapmaker

some sit at the altar of their mothers
sopping up her story
as it drips from her lips and limbs
but this is not our way

our mother is writing a new story
making it up as she goes
gathering things to pour
in the meantime

gentle strokes on my forearms
her touch is a balm
while we watch perfectly scripted lives
play out on screen

tethered by our longing
for a new story all our own
she reminds me
of my beauty and brains

laying solid ground in case
those holes need filling
she reminds us to stay open
never judge another

to look for those who need a kind friend
and be that
these are the lessons she's learned
that are becoming her story

that she's making with us
a story we are writing together
our little family
my mother is changing her stars
and we are her universe.

so grateful
for your resilience
and willingness to stay
so that i could have my person

and for knowing
you never regretted
those extra impossible years
because he was worth the risk

this perfect baby
my baby brother
my first best friend
my forever love.

—thanks mom

i watched my mother
fold out of herself
more times than there are
stars in the sky
and still somehow
she left enormous pieces
the best of herself
untouched
just for us.

—singin' giving you the best that i got, baby

gently greased parts
pressed by picks
and weathered fingertips
commanding grips
on cast iron skillets
deep inhales between
the hymns of a blessed spiritual
it is in these sacred spaces
of the southern woman
where god lives.

something about southern girls
who become southern women
like how heavy rain
turns to lightning storms
in a flash

red clay seeps into the bloodstream
and makes our hips sway
to the rhythm of the riverbed
cracks open our hearts so we can
keep conversation with the moon

—a direct line to the divine

TGIF

everything i see
inside that square screen
i want

the funny dad
who's always home for dinner
and looks lovingly at his beloved wife

the mom who moves with ease
with time for girl talk
and my midday school play

perfect obedient hair
cool clothes, clear skin
an even clearer identity

a house with stairs
and a bedroom the size of our apartment
that i don't have to share

all my dreams live
inside the wooden box
in the living room

one day i'mma dive deep
into that TV
and live a real life

nothing like
the pretend one
i live here.

i know my daddy loves me.

i know my daddy struggles
and that he means well.

i know my daddy is brilliant
and that he wants to do better.

i know my daddy regrets
a lot of things.

i know my daddy tries
to forgive himself.

i know my daddy
misses us.

but i do not know my daddy.

whose am i
if you never
came home
to claim me.

dear ~~god or santa or whoever keepin eyes on~~ **daddy,**

this morning you were asleep
on a mattress under the christmas tree
wearing your red shirt with the buttons
my favorite to dress up in
when you leave it/us behind
i carefully climbed in next to you
tucked myself under your arm
you are loud when you sleep
but you don't move
like you haven't rested in too many moons
like you are afraid of the dark too
and must stay awake with your back to the wall
just like you taught me
so as to keep eyes on the demons
that insist on moving in or on
every time you try to get right
i squeeze my head up under your chin
and drape one arm and leg over your body
this is my favorite way to rest
you are my favorite place
when you are still enough to hold
and now i know santa is real
because here you are, my dad
asleep under the christmas tree
just like i asked for in my letter.

i wonder where my mother buried her tongue
that she could live so many years
staring at our identical eyes
love us through our familiar fury
and never speak ill of you
how did she hold such sacred space
for a love that almost destroyed her?

why do my words always
make their way back to you
when there is no story there
you just weren't around
and even if you had been
it wouldn't change the fact
that you've always been
more comfortable
with distant apologies
than awkward presence
even when that space was held
by a wide open heart
holding up a sign
with your name on it.

in retrospect i understand
how you must have felt
to have demons bigger
than your natural capacity
i understand not knowing
how to choose yourself
from deep inside
the hole of dependence.

what i don't understand
is how you could go
so many days
years and years
wondering who your daughter was
when you could have simply shown up
and seen for yourself.

—*don't you know i worshiped the broken bits too*

daydreamin' daddy's girl

it amazes me
that after all the pain
you left me to drown in
if you were to walk through that door
my body would involuntarily
hurl itself towards yours
and my arms would melt around you
like a favorite memory that doesn't exist.

sixteen candles

my father showed up
to my high school graduation
with a bible.

i hadn't laid eyes on him
in over 10 years
just the random message
delivered through the grapevine.

he never answered a single secret birthday wish
by busting through the front door
right as i blow out the candles
to yell with all the love
he'd saved up just for me...

> *surprise, baby girl!*
> *i'd never forget you on your birthday!*

he just showed up.
with a bible.
one of those study ones

and i thought, how dare he?
or maybe i didn't think that at all
and the first time i repeated this story
that was someone else's reaction
so i made it my own.

i don't know.

because now, looking back
i think he was trying to tell me
something he'd learned in recovery

that if i'm going to survive
i need to believe in something.
i need something to anchor myself too.
and to trust him, he would know.

or maybe, he just thought
it was a good idea for me to stay studying.

or maybe, it was just a suggestion
and what he wanted to say was...

> *i'm not sure what you're into but...start here.*
> *it saved me in AA.*

or maybe,
it was the only thing
he could find at the gas station
on the way to the ceremony.

i don't know.

but i wish i had kept track of it.
if just to have some piece
of something he gave me
other than these bowed legs
this red hot temper
and an everlasting ache
for an unrealized love.

burn

mesmerized by the flame
i lit a match when i was four
and almost burned
our trailer to the floor

that's when i learned
something meant to warm
could also destroy

that some folks must be fire

and now i wonder
if that's why i am
covered in scars

from so many burns
dozens of marks
proofs of pain
from people
that i don't even remember.

"it ain't the brown that piss them off, baby
it's the Black that make you that way.
no matter how high yella you get
remember, you always a Black girl
and ain't nothing bigger than that."

–that time auntie gave me wings

this song goes out to the uncles of fatherless girls

one time for the uncles
of us fatherless girls
who pick us up in cadillacs
and ride to the beach or the corner store
when daddy don't show

one time for the uncles
who stay up late
talking shit and telling stories
of times they never put in books
cracking jokes and leaving footprints

one time for the uncles
who slip us secret c-notes
folded in giant, worn-out hands
that hold onto ours just long enough
to let you know they got you

one time for the uncles
of us fatherless girls
growing up surrounded by men meant to harm
but when standing wrapped in the arms
of my father's brother, we prosper

no weapon shall form against us.

act

2

(a story)

COLD OPEN

INT. HER BEDROOM, MARCH 2000 - LATE NIGHT

the moment she'd been afraid of / for all those years / the thing he'd been slowly escalating toward / since before she was 12 / waiting for the right opportunity / is here.

she is asleep until she isn't / she is in her room / he is not in his / his touch wakes her / but she doesn't move.

> HER THOUGHTS
> i'm confused, stay still and think
> i don't know what to do, stay still, think
> what will he do if i move, stay still
> what will i do if i move, stay still
> baby brother is in the next room, think
> there's no escape, just be still
> and try not to die

he is there for what feels like hours / but according to the clock she can only see in the periphery / through the tiny slither of her tightly shut eye / time has bent and it's only been minutes

> HER THOUGHTS
> keep your eyes closed, stay still, and quiet
> maybe it's better to go in peace

the last bit of silence she has / saved up / spent in those minutes.

he finishes and leaves / the scent of a predator disguised as a stepfather permanently stained / on her most sensitive skin

the split is complete / eternally severed from the girl she used to be / the her she used to know / with no time / for a proper goodbye.

END OF COLD OPEN

"if you wanna fly
you gotta give up the shit
that weighs you down."

–*Toni Morrison*

there once was a guy
named *"dad"*
he wasn't mine
but all i had
at first, he was cool
but then he turned cruel
and eventually, it all went bad.

—alternative way to tell this stepdad story

whole world in his hands

what makes you
want my small
shapeless body

or to show me your
grotesque bits
to no end

what makes you
so full of greed
and appetite

that even when
you have access
to literally everything

the whole world
contorted
to your will

you still
want
this tiny piece

of my entirety.

a deal with the devil

with the daily expectation of torment
comes a unique mercy i'd grown grateful for
my mind and body developed a routine
each playing a part in the performance
the predictability disguised as safety.

so when suddenly after the ten trillion days
that everyone else calls adolescence
to hear my bedroom door creek open
and smell the scent of alcohol and adult
closer than it'd ever been
at such an obscene hour
while mom was away
felt like an unlivable unfairness
for even the most seasoned sufferer.

what a fool i am
this deep in the game
to think his madness had limits
and that i had seen the extent of it.

my mama don't trust me
even though she don't know
the secrets i keep
and i don't blame her
if i'm awake
i'm lyin.

—thank god mama too busy lovin to notice

i know how to keep safe out there
but where's the after-school special
about what keeps me safe in here.

-*H.O.M.E.*

now i lay me down to sleep

speak up, girl
my god, say somethin!
she is right there
he's at work all night

hurry!
before the sun comes up
and it's too late again

hurry!
before you shrivel up
and disappear again

remember...
predators will switch course
to find their prey

a beast must feast
and your little brother
is asleep in the next room.

dope boy lullaby

i get more sound sleep
napping on the tattered couches
of trap houses
surrounded by brothers
who were barely boys
left to fend for themselves
than i do in tightly wrapped,
flower-printed comforters
bought for me with 45 minute commutes
and hard-earned direct deposits
feet from the room
my mama shares with that man.

four final days of forever

it's the morning
my body tried to rest
but my brain wouldn't let it

it's time to get dressed
i can't feel the clothes rake
over my unwashed skin

i walk outside the house
past his truck that has a fresh dent
on the bumper, a clue

driving myself to school
i consider my plan to survive one more night
with my mother still out of town

i'll ask a friend to sleep over
say it's some kind of emergency
he'll be too afraid to say no

as a backup i sneak away to ask M
to come by my window like he sometimes does
he looks at me strange when we speak, he knows

avoid people as much as possible
fake illness, have lunch in the production room
don't eat, skip practice, try to stop feeling sick

after school he asks me to drive him somewhere
his truck is gone, that's right, the dent
put it together, he drove drunk on the way to me?

consider running off the road
do the math, what would it take
to send him through the windshield but keep myself intact

consider if it's worth the risk
to just send both our bodies into that giant light pole
so this years long secret can be buried with us

return home to act out the plan
friend stays the night and M stops by window anyway
he says he just wanted to check, he knows

mom comes back in the morning
by then i have a new plan to get away and think
i call it a sleepover but go to the beach with J

J gets a motel room where we spend the night silent
in the morning he gets us breakfast and i call K
he's far away at college so i tell him everything

K gives me 24 hours to tell mom before he does
as soon as the conversation is over i can't remember it
but i know it happened because i miss the deadline

the next day at work i get a call from K
i collapse in the back room and get help to my car
he told her everything he could, she knows

i get home and it feels like a funeral
i confirm and cry and it's the worst hours yet
he's at work, the police are on their way

two cops come and i talk to the woman
as soon as the conversation is over i can't remember it
but i know it happened because of my decision

i've been 18 for 18 days
old enough to decide, too old to protect
i just want to graduate, go to college, and forget all this

i tell that to lady cop whose seen me cheer at football games
and noticed my name next to track stats in newspapers
she reminds me this process is not kind or quick, like on tv

with permission she paints a picture for the next year
repeated trips to a home i'm eager to put behind me
to sit on stands and retell stories and disclose partners,
etc. etc.

she says it can sometimes feel like it hasn't stopped
i thank her for that because it's all i needed to hear
i decide i'll have justice some other way

i pray regret won't swallow me whole
mom makes the call and takes care of the rest
i never have to see him again

except of course in dreams and memories that will take years
to slowly return in full color, arriving in bursts to each sense
catching me off guard on dates and in stores or mid-embrace

it feels weird to be charged with the labor of righting
the wrongs
when all i want is to live outside the shadow of him, for once
get to know people, move freely around my home, in my body

maybe that could be my justice.

in more than 2222 days
i never cried
it wasn't until i saw
what the weight of knowing
did to my mother
that my 2222 plus days
worth of tears
came pouring out
in a fiery flood
and almost drowned us both.

—thank god for those swim lessons

i watched my mama
get KO'd by heartbreak
*(by a closed fist too once
but that was a different time)*

her limp, lifeless body
swallowed up
by a thundercloud of shame

oh, it was terrifying
knowing all she'd done
to piece herself together

all the beatings she'd survived
from broken homes
and strung out men

what a fete it had been

only to be suckerpunched
by the same love
she thought saved her

and if it could happen to her
a living, breathing unicorn
it could surely happen to me.

—beware.

i pierced my tongue
on the night of my high school graduation
in a tiny tattoo parlor in Ybor City.

i pierced my tongue
hours after seeing my father
for the first time in over a decade.

i pierced my tongue
two months after revealing the 'terrible awful'
and ending a years-long era of abuse.

i wonder if i pierced my tongue
as punishment for speaking up
but still not saying so many unsaid things.

baby's first day of therapy

conjured from an hour of sick sorcery
casting spells on lifeless ears
and calling it healing
abandoned by a timekeeper
left to manage a furious comedown
whispering incoherent screams
in a fog of rage
i put my fist
through a glass frame
at the mere mention of his name

later i sat numbed and empty
while the nurse stitched
my bleeding wrist
not from an attempt to harm myself
but from throwing punches at a ghost
that still haunts the halls i call home

i should've known better than
to expect a man i never asked for
to help me heal
what a man i never asked for
had done

or maybe i'm only old enough
for the terrible
but not old enough
for the talking about it.

INT. MY MIND - NIGHT

the dreams are back again
i go home for break
thrilled to see my family
and he's there

they're all carrying on
as if everything is fine
or worse
as if they know
and don't care

i spend days screaming
exposing him for
exposing himself to me
and still they carry on

it gets harder
to contain myself.

finally, the rage wins.

i collapse into my animal self
a hyena-like creature
and i rip them all to shreds
with my claw-covered hands
and razor-sharp teeth.

i scream and cry
sitting in their bits of flesh
overcome with regret
desperately trying
to piece them back together again
so we can talk.

except him,
i save his parts
and set fire to them.

FADE TO BLACK.

why teach *me* to be vigilant
instead of teaching *him*
to **not** be dangerous.

Purple is The Color of forgiveness

on a recent pilgrimage to rural Georgia / a ritual to honor the patron saints of picture shows and the sacred scripture they brought to life / that guided me to and through early dialogues with the most high / up through Shug / down to Miss Sophia / all the way 'round to Nettie / and back where it all started / the hardest heart to hold for being too close to home / Miss Celie / i swear i heard her call to me / asking if i had considered forgiveness // so i reread the holy text / the pages that birthed a story i revisit like a real life relative / rooted to each others experience / she said: *look at me and Mister.*

maybe i do long for his atonement / her willingness to make space for it / could that be my path to mercy / some never-to-be-realized dream scenario / a day when that man would materialize / humble and pathetic / unable to make much of himself under the weight of his gross wrongdoing / barely able to stand before me / withering away / his limbs turning to gray ash / the terror on his face as he drifted into the wind / only able to be saved by my generous grace / then using the patience i learned under him / i wait for the last *please* / just before his disgusting lips fade away / and all that's left is that terrible hand that started it all / i reach up and grab his frail fingers / crushing them in my steady hand / then i pour those pitiful remains in the tiniest, airless vile / and say just loud enough for only god and what's left of his spirit to hear before it disappears into the great beyond: *there. now i have a piece of you.*

i guess i am no Celie / but then, he was no Mister / more like Pa / and anyway / i never pass a purple flower without praying thanks / so maybe if that stays true / and i stay good with the maker of the flowers and the me that sees the beauty / i don't need to forgive that man.

dear god

i wanted to give up today
and didn't
so

i guess you are out there
somewhere.

good southern girls
wear stockings
and secret-stained lips
when we talk to god

act

2

(b story)

dear god,

please help me stop stealing. it would be terrible to miss prom because i'm rotting in a cell for stealing three bras and a pair of bootcut Guess jeans. lord knows, i guess you know, my mom would leave me there to learn my lesson. but i don't think there's anything to learn. i'd happily use my lil' part time job money to pay for it if...i'm lyin again. sorry.

i like improving my technique. half the stuff i don't even wear. i just let girls borrow it who i know won't give it back and the scales feel balanced again. if only i had a healthy hobby to put this energy—i know you don't like the other thing i do to release. i don't know, man, i mean god. sorry. maybe if i could get back whatever was stolen from me i'd stop taking things from department stores and heal.

thank you for ~~weed, kissing, and oatmeal pies~~ my mama, my grandma, and my baby brother.

i'm sorry, i'll try to stop.

amen.

growing up
most of my prayers
were negotiations

the first time
i felt the confusing fire
between my legs
was just before recess
on picture day

the mix of curiosity
and fight
being held down
by my classmate's small body
watching my pink dress
with the black stripes
my favorite
rise higher than i knew
it was allowed to go

the uncertainty silenced me
the attention excited me
after a couple of moments
we were caught
by our 1st grade teacher
and i'll never forget...

after she beat him
with the wooden paddle
that hung on the side of her desk
before laying into
my same backside
that'd been pressed into the floor
under the weight of us both
she said,
at full volume,
looking only at me:

—YOU SHOULD KNOW BETTER

kissin' you

i had my first real kiss today
that other one in the backseat of the hearse on a dare
with too-tight lips and no tongue didn't count

it was awkward and kind of terrible
in front of too many people.

i think from now on i'll only kiss where no one can watch
i'll keep my eyes open so i can see his intention

i thought we would ease into it like in the movies
pulled together by some gentle irresistible force
but it was hard-pressed, mouth wide open from jump

he tasted nice though
like now and laters, sprite and sweetness
but now i'm worried about my own taste

doing anything for the first time is scary
but doing something instead of having it done to me
is new and strange

kissing who i want is cool but i think
it's more complicated than i thought

i like him but i don't like kissing him like that
next time i'll start and show him what i want

or maybe 7th grade will end before i have to do it again

it's weird...to still have so many firsts
when i already feel used up.

pretty for a Black girl

you kinda like my light skin
it brings you relief
when you're drawn to Blackness
you relish my in-between

you swing open the door
expecting to find an easy time
never considering
Black is my forever bottom line

you breeze past the kinks
say you like how i move my hips
trying to steal secret kisses
boy, these ain't my mama lips

i see you makin' sense of it
you can trust what feels whyte
you think it gives you favor
when it should give you fright

see i've learned over the years
some dark and some not
this piece of privilege we share
it costs you a whole lot

it's delusion, dear boy
these supreme lie things
your people betrayed you
you're the one with clipped wings.

duality

it is a strange
phenomenon
to feel both heavy
and hollowed out
in the same
small body.

(de)flowers don't drop petals

the first time i made
the choice for myself
i was shocked by how
little i felt afterward
staring at myself
in the bathroom mirror
searching for difference
maturity
appeal
love
but all i saw
were the same
stone eyes looking back
wondering if i'd lost all right
to the magic of moments
meant to mean something
and how to get this used up boy
out of my mother's house
before she wakes up.

i suppose having to sift
every encounter
environment
every single moment
through a filter of vigilance
a thorough risk assessment
is the most stifling of the things
after all, seems i should be able
to do / speak / decide / be
without always wondering
what offense it might cause you
and what harm it might cause me.

being a "virgin"
has never meant more
than knowing the difference
between being a "good girl"
and being good, girl.

pleasure principle

i do it when i should be studying
or finishing homework due yesterday
i do it when i should be resting
for races i'll win come saturday
i do it in the backseats of cars
and in clearings in orange groves
i do it on the floors of boys bedrooms
they'll clean over the weekend
while their exhausted mothers fold
laundry listening to Anita Baker
i do it quietly on the floor of my own bedroom
after everyone's asleep and i've learned
to open the window undetected
i do it because i can
and i want to learn to like it
i must practice pleasure
fake it 'til i make it
mine again.

the case of the disappearing virgins

when in circles
of girls my age
but not my experience
i talk about sex
real casual like
never putting much
weight in the act
and only the feeling
after the fact

so when the virgins
come to me
too afraid
to be shamed
by their actual friends
i tell them the same tale
around camp bonfires
real-life ghost stories

do what you want
but only if you want
because done any other way
you'll disappear
never to be heard from again.

as early as 9th grade
they stick us in home ec
and teach us how to make
an upside-down pineapple cake
because the key to a boy's heart
depends on how well you can satiate

but these boys become men no matter how well they're fed
who seem to never fill and become ravenous instead
so i think maybe there could be some class like art
that shows them how to fill their own broken hearts
so when the world leaves holes they can grab
a paintbrush and not even think
to reach for any of us.

i wonder what it is
that makes you want
so much more when
i have emptied myself out
in offering to you.

-16 year old boys have big appetites

mama said, mama said

i hear her judgment
and take it personal
as if to say i
improperly love
as if she could be
one to tell me
i shout

he's not my boyfriend!

a weak defense
excusing his
repeated wrongdoing
or maybe my own
and my mother
etches in me
forevermore

*you must be right because
that boy is no friend of yours.*

let him eat cake

each time you step out
to find some easier
more adoring version of me
you will find yourself wanting

you'll soon learn
i cannot be duplicated
nothing simple can be made
in my image

you ate good
but didn't leave
with the recipe

makes me wonder
what will become of that girl
once you start to punish her
for her blandness
and your longing

makes me wonder
who you punish me for.

dust yourself off and try again

that first time
after the terrible awful
under the starry night sky
because beds made me
sick for so long
the scent of freshly cut grass
and invisible open wounds
still lingering in the air
i asked you to
treat me like normal
and i learned
when asking for
what i want
to be specific
because i didn't
want our normal
i wanted
gentle
healing
love
something we
had never done.

no offense

sometimes i wish you'd die
not an actual death
just some kind of accident

you take a hit on the field
and it only affects the part
of your brain where i live

you remember your mama
her red velvet cake and your sister's
sweetness but not me

you won't recognize my face
you forget the way i walk
the smell of me fades

it'll be like i/we never existed
our on again off again
will end forever

erased from all memories
except for mine
you are too valuable to forget

your imprint will remain
that way i'm less likely
to go looking for you again.

to the girl in the mirror

even though his voice
was strong enough to save you
from the absence of yours

even though he did the right thing
said the impossible words
it took to make it all stop

you are not
bound to him
forever.

one massive good deed
does not erase that time
he spit in your face

love is not to be confused
with obligation
or gratitude

break up
with him.

boys + girls club

what makes them quiet our girls
only to amplify our boys
don't you want to know
the secrets of the universe.

i used to pray for a fat ass
and a smaller nose
so i could catch his eye
long enough to keep his interest
now all i wish
is that he would forget me.

i never loved you
you were just
a convenient place
to put my rage.

—thank you, ex

some roses grow best in concrete

i know that for sure because
an asphalt track and a field of teammates
was my most fertile ground

my feet were the sturdiest
standing between sisters
moving in unison on concrete sidelines

having a curve to lean into
a baton to pass off
a race to win
a time to beat
was oxygen

without the permission and place
to put feet to fire and forge forever bonds
i would have burnt up
instead i set blaze and new records

my creative force poured
into pep rallies and fed routine roots
burst through chants and out the ends
of sky-high toe touches

back and forth to practices
twice a day, sometimes more
stretched between one side
of the world to the other

i found space for the beast me
and turned rage into war chants
gold medals, championships,
and so. many. flowers.

how many of us have them?

friends are a tricky thing
when you can't be honest
about who you are

friends are complicated
when you never want to bring them home
because of the fear they might see
the real deal and expose you (to yourself)

friends' parents ask questions
you squirm while trying to answer
when you spend too much time at their house
but insist on returning because
you need to get home to your baby brother

friends are hard to keep
for longer than a year
when the identity you were wearing
has expired and everything attached to it
must die too

friends, the good ones anyway
want to know more than you're willing to tell
get closer than you're allowed to get
and require more than you have the capacity to give

friends are exhausting
when there's so much upkeep
they require trust and closeness
the two most impossible things

so i can be their friend
but they can't be mine
because no one can love something
that doesn't actually exist
and i have been gone
for quite some time

i do feel especially bad about that.

eulogy for my 1st boyfriend

MG died two days ago.
somebody who knew me when he was
my "boyfriend" for five minutes in 8th grade told me
i saw him just a few weeks ago for the first time
since that last week in middle school

he was only seventeen
a basketball star at another school
he smiled when he saw me in my cheer uniform
we caught up and talked shit like rival schools
in one of those musical movies

i wish i would've given him my number
so we could've had one last secret late-night talk
he could've told me everything
he wanted to do beyond basketball
and i would've told him how
i count the days to leave this place and go
(i don't tell anyone that)

at the funeral, his sister told a story
a conversation they had just days before the accident
he told her he was ready to go if called
said he wasn't scared of death and trusted god
i keep thinking about that

imagining the car hitting him
wondering if he immediately surrendered
they brought in therapists at all the high schools
but i didn't talk to them
i just spoke to the sky

i've never lost anyone but i think
there's a time when they can still hear you

i hope so because i want him to know
if he had anything left to give

he can channel it through me
and i promise to leave it all on the track
or the field or in the stands

enough for the both of us.

dances in vacant lots

skip class to cross town
pass blunts and black n milds
before cheer practice
cookin' rocks and throwin' bottles
needles and naysayers
penetration and penitentiaries
deployments and disappointments
broken hearts and bank accounts
so many versions
existing at once
it's easy to get turned around
or lost and forget which one
i'm allowed to be and where
sometimes cussing my way
through an 8 count
then crying into a box of broken-up herb
confusing which feeling goes where
since none of them live in me
inhospitable and running constantly
sometimes on tracks for medals
mostly inside and away from myself
unable to settle into a state
or a relationship
or an open book
terrified to study
worried if i sit still too long
something terrible will happen
or worse
someone might see me
for the shell i am.

what a boy you were
to make me feel safe when my
whole world was in flames

-haiku for the boy next door

holy grail

if i am a prayer
you are a meditation
i sit on your presence
listening
for your truth
and it comes
in all its glory.

i have met death
and been born again
so many times
my touch
is a christening
for weary souls
you enter
these pearly gates
to get baptized
with holy rose water
and revealed to yourself.

—do you like what you see?

pillow talk with a priestess

i ask her

*how do you do that
with your mouth?*

she smiles,
and i continue...

how do you speak so freely?

breadcrumbs for the beautiful girl i wanted to be/with

she tells me
she feels green
sometimes
when she looks
at my life
and i beg her:

please don't.
i didn't make it to someone else's
promise land but perpetually
10,000 steps shy of my own
in one piece

and some days
when no one is looking
all i do is retrace my steps
searching for bits of me
i lost along the way.

once upon a time

some girls get fairytales
knights on white horses
betrothed to brute force
and ideals of beauty

other girls get rituals of renewal
witchy covens to belong
black cauldrons, sacred spell books
and ancient artifacts

please god give me the magic
over the happy ending
i'd rather be a sorcerer
than somebody's princess.

things i like, for remembering

scrambled eggs and cheese grits
(add fish or corned beef hash out the can,
if available, and make it real special)
big ol' glasses of ice cold sweet tea
mac n cheese and collard greens
but not everybody's and especially grandma's
mama's ham and cabbage and carrot cake
freshly cut grass under my bare feet
we really like being barefoot
swimming in a pool on a hot night
splashing around where
the gulf waves meet powdery earth
funny people and pretty words
like extraordinary, constellations, and glory
gold teeth tucked between big soft lips
tiny jewelry caught on collar bones
and kinky curls and southern drawls
giant blankets and warm thighs
to tuck my toes and other things under
soft touches and hard laughs
laying under the stars
long baths and longer walks
sweet potato pie and a gentle breeze
big ol trees that feel like home
crab boils on late nights with good music
oysters with cocktail sauce on a saltine
soaking up sister sun on my face
falling asleep in her warm spot
flipping through a magazine
with nowhere to be and nothing else to do
dancing around to buju or zhané
remember i like this life
and so do you
stay.

the numbers are forever in my favor

by 18 there have been
9 schools between 3 cities and 7 homes
1 mother, 1 lost father, and 1 evil stepfather
1 beloved twin brother born 5 years younger
1 dream/2 distant sisters, all from the same mister
2 dead grandpas, 1 spirit grandma, 1 living force
77 months of torture, 1 breaking point
at least 143 kisses, some wanted, some not
3 "boyfriends", 6 practice partners, 1 lover, maybe 2
if you count the one secretly borrowed from a friend
3 fights, 1 suspension
1 black eye, unrelated
6 broken hearts
4 college acceptances
22 pep rallies
44 football games
1 tattoo, 4 piercings
2 national championships, 1 all-american
1 arrest, 6 months probation
4 hours drive to college
3 or more different versions of this one wild life
and counting.
praise be, and counting.

act

3

"sister, you been on my mind
sister, we're two of a kind
oh, sister, i'm keeping my eye on you."

–Shug Avery

there were times
when the pain seeped out
through unkept seams, sometimes
crushing spirits and hurting feelings.
sometimes in raised voices and flying objects.
there may have been some broken hearts
and for sure, blatant disrespect.
i am most sorry for this.

learn to be on time
with your presence
and your apologies
punctuality matters

dearest friend,

some call you dissociation,
i call you mercy.
my specific saving grace
god bless you.

my body welcomes me home

thank you, dear body
for knowing what to do
how to stay and stand
while i floated far away
or hid deep inside the split

divine mercy wrapped in
detachment and disguise
allowing me to become
separate for such long times
how lonely you were
how brutal i could be

thank you for finding ways
methods of release
even in rage and sorrow
you were gently tending
careful not to let the good
seep out of the busted seams

all in service
to keep us breathing
reminding us of the stories
we'd written of times
on the other side
promised by a great mystery

thank you
for patiently biding time
always holding space
for me to return home
so we could get busy
doing our divine work
of being alive.

graveyards

you are not the first
version of us i buried
there are thousands more
some with entire universes
dancing in our fingertips

i hid you deep down
beneath the muck
where we put things
we don't want seen
like bodies and secrets

or things we want kept safe
like bodies and secrets
i had no idea
it'd take this long to return
to sit and visit for a spell

to remember
our most sacred stories
to reclaim the me before him
i'm sorry, i never meant
to stay away so long

i am here now
and i will never
leave us again.

torn petals
dulled thorns
and bruised buds
a flower still makes

a rose is still a rose
even when it
stops blooming
for safety reasons.

i thought those years
had swallowed me whole

turns out
the belly of the beast
is ripe for growth

i made the madness
into a flowerbed

everything you took
i grew back tenfold.

sweet tea, phone home

before the concrete of the city
or the cool sand of the coast
you were birthed and bathed
in red clay.

your earth matters, country girl.

temple

here i was
searching
far and wide
only to find
the sanctuary
i seek was
within me.

my mother
grows softer with age

that's how i know
to equate ease to years lived.

i hope i live to be three hundred years old.

the armor helped me survive
but it was the softness
that saved me.

ruby slippers

i fell in love
somewhere over the rainbow
skipping eagerly down
anything resembling
a yellow brick road
only to find
like glenda the good witch said,

i had the power
all along.

the split

i heard you are still very much in your split. that space you live in between the you that faces the world and the you hidden away, waiting for a safe moment to surface. i know it's lonely, being disconnected from your body and mad as all get out but somewhere in the scary, it is sacred. specific knowing can be formed from living so deeply in your interior world. with survival comes lessons in alchemy: how to turn shadows into light, how to process pain into offering, how to live. your aliveness never leaves you. your breath shapeshifts into profound truths and self-awareness. you may even get glimpses of it in those deep soul breaths. just keep breathing. you won't be stuck forever. eventually, you will pour out from that same space meant to keep you from yourself. you will find your voice. whether it's shouts, whispers, or written words. it might feel foreign, wobbly, as it does for us once-caged birds, but with every word you speak, every bit of love and grace you show yourself you clear away some of the hardened bits and create space for all you buried or had stolen or sent away for safekeeping to come running home to you. it takes time but you have siblings along the journey. just look left or write and we're here with arms outstretched.

when i realized
healing is a practice

not a state

i stopped feeling
like a failure.

if i never told nobody but god
and my body still knows
what does that make me?

what does it make you?

dear girl,

you are made up of
star stuff and sweetness
no matter how many times
he deposits poison inside you.

xo

just because your pain doesn't come
in soft tears and gentle moans
and instead arrives hot and fast
doused in fury and fire
doesn't mean it isn't real
or deserving of love
and protection
you are simply
a holy inferno.

some will not be able
to withstand your truth
this might make you silent
the good news is
you grow out of that
with every word you speak.

—baby steps are still steps

playing small
never kept
anyone safe.

big is your birthright.

you know the rose
the one that grew from a crack
in the concrete
who defied the odds and gods
and sang its song
that's you
you are the rose.

mecca

if it's god you're worried about
here's a secret the deacons
with the wandering eyes
and too low back pats
won't tell you:

the closest to god
you'll ever be is
in your own body.

that same place the world
works so hard to make inhospitable
is a temple of the divine

to be in touch with yourself
rooted in your feminine essence
is to be on the holiest ground.

amazing grace

look for yourself in nature
when you feel lost or alone
look to the madness of lightning strikes
the still silence on a crisp fall day
find your fear in the same waves
meant to wash it away
run your worry right out of your pores
jumping from dirt mound to grassy patch

just go outside and see yourself.

and all the ways this planet
and the most high is telling you
there is room for all the parts
both the beauty and the decay
beyond the room to hold them,
look at them all working in harmony
with the highest divine purpose
to keep you alive.

our body leaves the light on

our life's work will be turning
our fragmented pieces to whole
we will seek out maps and
coordinates in the cosmos and learn
to follow the way the wind blows
only to find the imprint
of our origin self welcoming
us with a supernova-sized embrace
that's been there the whole time
singing our birth song
calling us home.

stay

there may come a time
when you want to stop feeling.
but please, resist.

feeling is the only way through
it keeps us connected to our essence
and reminds us we are alive

even when it's excruciating
because as painful as it can be
it is nothing, not even close
nowhere in the same realm,
compared to our aliveness

remember that you were
in agreement to be here
in this moment and
enough moments since

you don't need constant happy
that isn't real anyway
what matters is that you
keep making the choice
to stick around

and in return, this massive galaxy
that thought enough of you in the first place
keeps meeting you with open arms
offering literally everything
in exchange for your presence.

we write stories
of times never had
stories of superheroes
or magic men
monsters under the bed

we write stories
because we have none
or refuse the real ones
when they're too
painful to keep

we write stories
because we have to
our tales long forgotten
erased or replaced
and we need them

to feel whole
so we don't fill holes
with poison or people
or poison people
but we must fill to feel

so we write stories
and talk them forward
pass down tales
to sense the thing
we all crave to feel

–free

p.s.

your feelings are natural.
the weirdness, sensitivity, queerness,
thoughtfulness, curiosity, creativity
keep exploring.
you can be everything
or none of it, any day of the week
there is boundless beauty
in fluidity.
you are up to you.

trust yourself.
find **your** people.
believe in **magic**.

dearest reader,

if you hear the call of recovery or healing from a younger self,
answer. if i hadn't responded to the demand, i may have never
found poetry growing along the way. it turns out, there was magic
under the muck that helped me turn wounds into words.
then i used them to honor baby me, free current me,
and connect to you, dear friend.
thank you for traveling through space and time
on a fraction of the stories of my life.
if i could mail my love right to you, i would.
instead please accept this energetic sweetness, a salve
to apply wherever you felt pricked by the painful pieces.
i'm so grateful to you for journeying with me.
i hope you'll keep this book as the companion it was
intended to be as you move along your own path.
i can't wait to come back and share more. because as heavy as
much of those first 18 years were, the next bit was so damn good.
i'll see you on the page again soon.
in the meantime, as E.Badu said, *pack light.*
all you must hold on to, is you.

p.s. now that you know so much of my business,
we go together. real bad.

kiloveyoubye.

survivor support + mental health resources

RAINN: (Rape, Abuse & Incest National Network) is the nation's largest anti-sexual violence organization. RAINN created and operates the National Sexual Assault Hotline: 800-656-HOPE (4673), oneline.rainn.org

METOO: The 'me too.' movement works toward eradicating sexual violence by shifting culture, policies, and institutions. Text METOOACTION to 24020. metoomvmt.org

THE LOVELAND FOUNDATION: The Loveland Foundation brings opportunity and healing to communities of color, especially Black women and girls through fellowships, residency programs, listening tours, and more. thelovelandfoundation.org

TWLOHA: To Write Love on Her Arms is a non-profit movement dedicated to presenting hope and finding help for people struggling with depression, addiction, self-injury, and suicide. twloha.com

JOYFUL HEART FOUNDATION: Joyful Heart Foundation's mission is to transform society's response to sexual assault, domestic violence, and child abuse, support survivors' healing, and end this violence forever. joyfulheartfoundation.org

survivor support + mental health resources

988 SUICIDE + CRISIS LINE: The 988 lifeline provides 24/7, free and confidential crisis resources for you and loved ones. Call 988, 988lifeline.org

FORGE: Forge is a national transgender anti-violence organization that helps transgender, gender nonconforming, and gender nonbinary survivors of sexual assault. forge-forward.org

NATIONAL SEXUAL VIOLENCE RESOURCE CENTER: A national information and resource organization that works with the CDC to share resources with people and organizations working to understand and eliminate sexual violence. nsvrc.org

THERAPY FOR BLACK GIRLS: Therapy for Black Girls is an online space dedicated to encouraging the mental wellness of Black women and girls. therapyforblackgirls.com

THE TREVOR PROJECT: The Trevor Project is the leading suicide prevention organization for LGBTQ young people. Reach a trained counselor at 866-488-7386. thetrevorproject.org

SAFE HORIZON: Resources for survivors of domestic violence, human trafficking, child abuse, stalking, and youth homelessness. safehorizon.org

acknowledgments

i'll try to keep this shorter than the acceptance speech i've been rehearsing in the shower since i was 12...

to my mother, my first forever home, i'll love you forever, i'll like you for always. you're the reason i know we can change our stars. my brother, my first baby, and my absolute favorite person on the planet and best friend. i could fill 10 books with love poems for the two of you.

my grandma for always keeping us covered in prayer and support, for treating mom like your own, and for loving us in a way only you can. you're my favorite girl. my aunts and uncles for their guidance, gems, and joy. thank you for filling the empty spots, i'm more whole because of it. to the coolest big/little sister, thank you for always making me feel like i belonged. sisters and cousins who traded dixie cups for star crunches at stevens park, played music i'd fall in love with, and made sure i always felt like family no matter how long it'd been, i love y'all.

mr. smith, thank you for holding space for me to time travel and for gently pulling me back to the present when i needed it. sometimes i see baby tiff grinning back at me from the twinkle in your eye—you knew her biggest dream before i did and then you made it come true, thank you. in all the timelines.

my two hearts, for mirroring back the best of me especially when revisiting versions who had no idea how good things would turn out. you two are the very best thing, my favorite story.

the warm and wonderful people who teach, guide, and look after my two hearts every day so i can focus on my work, you are a gift. we love you. to our ATX community—near and far—thank you for co-caring and feeding and loving—especially when i'm at capacity and without judgement. y'all da best.

friends who read pages, talk for hours, and remind me that among the many things, i am, in fact, a writer—'preciate you big. thank you for saving me millions on talk therapy and hard drugs. and for being my familiar in foreign places and staying my friend even though it pretty much guarantees i'll write about you.

to those who helped hold some of these stories over the years with such gentle care, thank you for seeing the me beyond the pain. for growing wider arms to embrace all the parts and for seeing me, especially when i couldn't see myself. and for your specific significance in my healing, Js, you *take me to the place i love*. our story got next.

since so many of these pieces were born from revisiting a specific set of years, they require a specific set of acknowledgments:

track coaches who pushed, protected, and cared, cheer coaches who felt like friends, especially the one who saw more in me, an honest history teacher, the kindest science teacher, a radical english teacher.

a squad of sisters who i loved best i could and who loved me back, 4x1 team who meant more than i knew how to show. friends made in the Meadows, girlfriends who spent hours driving to the beach and eating entire sheet cakes, practicing routines, sharing clothes and secrets, their homes and parents and selves–thank god for you. it all felt real even if i wasn't.

curious girls and discreet boys who were lovers turned friends and vice versa, it wasn't nothing to practice safety with you. there was so much love and learning, i promise to never use any of your real names. to the bravest, most brutal boy who broke my spirit but saved my life, i'm forever grateful.

everyone who looked out for, accepted, and loved me–in middle and high school, especially–you helped me breathe. thank you, thank you, thank you.

author in her natural habitat

tiffany rose is a storyteller and somebody's mama. she loves elephants and 90s reruns. she's a pisces with an Oprah rising and believes the key to life is to trust yourself, find your people, and believe in magic. and that snacks and falling in love with as many things as possible are of equal importance. she's online at rosewithwords.com or on the apps @rosewithwords (but she's really only ever on instagram). you can also find her in a library sniffing books or taking long walks under trees near water.

Made in the USA
Monee, IL
25 September 2023

43365606R00083